Finding Your Circles of Passion: Crafting a Purposeful Life

Marako Marcus

Published by Marako Marcus, 2023.

Introduction: Finding Your Circles of Passion - Crafting a Purposeful Life

In the tapestry of human existence, purpose serves as the guiding thread that weaves together our aspirations, actions, and endeavors. It is the driving force behind our decisions, the source of our motivation, and the beacon that illuminates our path. Finding purpose is a quest that resonates deep within each of us, a journey that can lead us to profound fulfillment and a life rich with meaning. Welcome to "Finding Your Circles of Passion: Crafting a Purposeful Life," a transformative journey that will empower you to unlock the intricate map of purpose within you.

"From the spark of passion emerges the flame of purpose."

The Power of Purposeful Living

Throughout history, individuals have sought to uncover the elusive concept of purpose – that intangible force that gives depth and significance to our existence. Purpose transcends the mundane routines of life; it invites us to tap into our unique talents, passions, and aspirations. It is the anchor that keeps us grounded in turbulent times and the fuel that propels us toward our dreams.

As the author of this book, drawing from over 25 years of experience in consulting and coaching, I've had the privilege of witnessing firsthand the transformative impact of purposeful living. I've walked alongside individuals as they navigated the labyrinth of their lives, guiding them to discover their passions, align with their values, and carve out their own paths of fulfillment. Now, I am excited to extend this journey to you – an invitation to explore, reflect, and embark on a voyage of self-discovery.

Mapping Your Purpose: The Circles of Passion

Imagine your life as a canvas, awaiting the vibrant strokes of purpose to paint a masterpiece. This book introduces a novel approach to finding and cultivating your purpose: the concept of "Circles of Passion." Each of the circles presented within this book represents a distinct facet of human experience, a realm where purpose can flourish and bloom. From social justice to music engagement and sustainable agriculture, these circles encompass a diverse array of possibilities, tailored to different passions and inclinations.

Each circle represents a realm of passion waiting to be explored. By delving into these circles, you will embark on a journey of self-discovery, revealing the aspects of life that resonate most deeply with your heart and soul. As you engage with each chapter, you will uncover opportunities to infuse your existence with purpose, whether by nurturing your love for animals, fostering relationships, embracing entrepreneurship, or engaging in artistic expression.

A Personal Odyssey: Navigating Your Unique Path

One of the remarkable aspects of this exploration is the acknowledgment of our individuality. Just as fingerprints are distinct, so too are the Circles of Passion that resonate within us. No two journeys will be identical; the circles that hold profound significance for you may differ from those that speak to others. It is this diversity that makes the quest for purpose all the more captivating and enriching.

This book invites you to embark on your own personal odyssey, an expedition into the landscapes of your passions, values, and dreams. Your purposeful journey begins by reading through the circles presented within this book, identifying the ones that strike a chord within your heart. As you navigate these chapters, take the time to assess your own satisfaction level within each circle. Consider the significance it holds for you and the impact it has on your life.

Crafting a Purposeful Life: Your Adventure Awaits
At the heart of this book lies the invitation to create a meaningful life by intentionally cultivating the Circles of Passion that resonate with you. Just as a gardener tends to a garden, nurturing each plant with care, you too have the power to nurture and develop the circles that ignite your spirit. As you embark on this journey, you will find guidance, inspiration, and practical insights to help you deepen your engagement with these circles.

Remember that life is a dynamic and ever-changing tapestry. Just as seasons shift, so too will your Circles of Passion evolve. Life stages, experiences, and growth will influence the circles that hold the most significance for you. Embrace the ebb and flow of this journey, and allow yourself the grace to adapt and explore new circles as you traverse the landscape of your existence.

As you delve into the chapters that follow, I encourage you to approach each circle with an open heart and a curious mind. Engage in introspection, self-assessment, and action. Your journey toward a more purposeful life begins now. With this book as your guide, you have the tools to craft a life that is not only rich with purpose but also uniquely and authentically your own.

Navigating Your Self-Assessment: The Importance-Satisfaction Matrix

The Importance-Satisfaction Matrix: Unveiling Your Landscape Imagine your purposeful journey as a vast terrain, dotted with the Circles of Passion you've encountered in this book. Each circle holds unique significance to you, shaping the contours of your existence. To navigate this landscape, we'll employ a two-dimensional map: the Importance-Satisfaction Matrix.

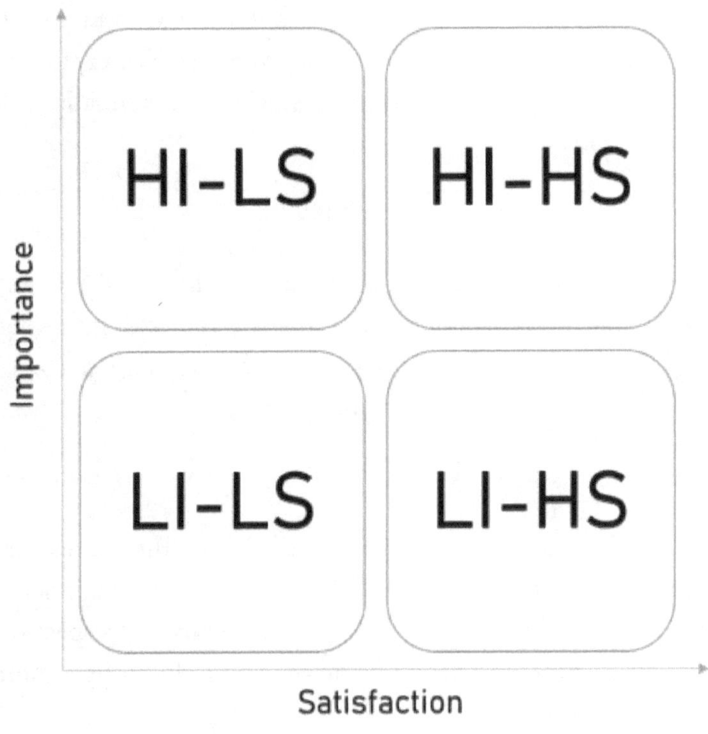

In this matrix, you'll find four distinct zones:

High Importance, High Satisfaction (HI-HS): These circles are the jewels of your purposeful journey. They align with your core values and bring you deep fulfillment. Cultivate and nurture these circles to continue experiencing profound joy and meaning.

High Importance, Low Satisfaction (HI-LS): These circles hold significant importance to you, but you may find your current engagement less satisfying. This zone invites you to explore ways to enhance your experience within these circles, potentially unlocking untapped potential.

Low Importance, High Satisfaction (LI-HS): While these circles may not hold paramount importance, your current engagement brings you great satisfaction. Continue to enjoy and celebrate these circles, allowing them to enrich your journey.

Low Importance, Low Satisfaction (LI-LS): These circles may not currently resonate deeply with you, and your engagement might not be particularly satisfying. This zone encourages introspection – is it time to release these circles, or could there be hidden opportunities for growth within them?

Using the Matrix: Navigating Your Purposeful Landscape
To harness the power of the Importance-Satisfaction Matrix, follow these steps:

Reflect on Each Circle: Take time to consider each circle presented in this book. How important is it to you? How satisfied are you with your current engagement in it?

Plot Your Circles: Place each circle within the matrix based on its importance and your satisfaction level. Trust your intuition and be honest with yourself.

Explore Each Zone: Once you've plotted your circles, explore each zone – HI-HS, HI-LS, LI-HS, and LI-LS. Embrace curiosity as you ponder why certain circles fall into each category.

Action and Intention: For circles in the HI-LS zone, consider how you can elevate your satisfaction. Explore opportunities to deepen your engagement, seek new experiences, or acquire new skills. For circles in the LI-HS zone, recognize their positive impact and continue to relish in their contributions. Reflect on circles in the LI-LS zone – are there aspects that could bring more satisfaction, or is it time to reallocate your energy?

E mbrace the Ebb and Flow
Remember, your landscape of purpose is dynamic, evolving as you journey through different life stages and experiences. What resonates deeply today may evolve over time. As you engage with the Importance-Satisfaction Matrix, embrace the ebb and flow of your purposeful journey. Adapt, explore, and transform with each step you take.

As you proceed through this book, allow the Importance-Satisfaction Matrix to be your compass, guiding you toward a life rich with meaning and fulfillment. Your purposeful journey is a symphony of circles, and within each note lies the potential to craft a harmonious masterpiece.

Chapter 1: Social Justice

Description: Social Justice involves standing up for causes, promoting equality, and driving positive change in society. This circle empowers you to be a force of transformation and a voice for those who may not have one. Examples include advocating for gender equality, racial justice, and environmental conservation.

Self-Assessment Questions:
How important is advocating for social justice and driving positive change to you? (1-10)

How satisfied are you with your current level of involvement in social justice efforts? (1-10)

Tips and Ideas:
Join local activist groups and NGOs to amplify your impact.

Engage in awareness campaigns through social media and community events.

Volunteer your time for causes that resonate with you deeply.

Educate yourself about different social justice issues to be a more informed advocate.

Collaborate with like-minded individuals to organize workshops and seminars.

Chapter 2: Community Engagement

Description: Community Engagement involves actively participating and contributing to local and global communities. This circle encourages you to connect with others, collaborate on initiatives, and make a positive impact in your surroundings. Examples include volunteering for community clean-up events, supporting local businesses, and organizing neighborhood projects.

Self-Assessment Questions:

How important is actively engaging with your community and making a positive impact to you? (1-10)

How satisfied are you with your current level of involvement in community activities and projects? (1-10)

Tips and Ideas:

Join community events, town hall meetings, and volunteer opportunities to connect with locals.

Organize community-based projects, such as neighborhood gardens or art installations.

Support local businesses by shopping locally and participating in "shop small" initiatives.

Create online platforms or social media groups to facilitate community discussions and events.

Collaborate with community leaders and organizations to address pressing local issues.

Chapter 3: Tabletop Games and Play

Description: Immerse yourself in the world of tabletop games, where strategy, camaraderie, and a touch of friendly competition come together to create memorable bonding experiences. Examples include playing classic board games, exploring the joy of card games such as poker and bridge.

Self-Assessment Questions:

How important is the act of tabletop games and play in your life?

How satisfied are you with your current level of engagement with tabletop games?

Tips and Ideas:

Host game nights to foster connections and create lasting memories.

Explore various genres of games, from cooperative to competitive, to find what suits your preferences.

Attend gaming conventions and events to discover new games and connect with fellow enthusiasts.

Create your custom rules or variations for existing games to add a personal touch.

Use tabletop games as an opportunity for team-building and problem-solving exercises.

Chapter 4: Gaming Interest (Online, Mobile, Virtual)

Description: Gaming Interest involve finding purpose and fulfillment through video games, mobile games and gaming communities. This circle empowers you to explore different game genres, connect with fellow gamers, and engage in competitive or collaborative gameplay. Examples include participating in game tournaments, creating gaming content, and exploring virtual, augmented reality worlds.

Self-Assessment Questions:

How important is engaging in gaming as a source of entertainment, community, and personal growth to you? (1-10)

How satisfied are you with your current level of involvement in gaming and gaming-related activities? (1-10)

Tips and Ideas:

Explore a variety of game genres to discover what resonates with your interests.

Join gaming forums, online communities, or social media groups to connect with fellow gamers.

Participate in local or online game tournaments to challenge your skills and meet new people.

Create games, such as streaming or videos, to share your experiences and insights.

Participate in games that are activity based to maintain a healthy lifestyle.

Chapter 5: Professional Career Growth

Description: Professional Career Growth involves pursuing a fulfilling and impactful career that aligns with your passions and goals. This circle empowers you to continuously learn and develop your skills to advance in your chosen field. Examples include setting career goals, pursuing higher education, and building a strong professional network.

Self-Assessment Questions:

How important is achieving career growth and pursuing a fulfilling professional path to you? (1-10)

How satisfied are you with your current career trajectory and professional development efforts? (1-10)

Tips and Ideas:

Set clear career goals and create a roadmap for achieving them.

Seek out opportunities for continuous learning and skill development.

Attend conferences, workshops, and networking events to expand your connections.

Offer mentorship to junior colleagues and seek guidance from experienced professionals.

Consider pivoting your career if your current path doesn't align with your passions and goals.

Chapter 6: Managerial Responsibilities

Description: Managerial Responsibilities involve leading and managing teams, projects, and organizations effectively. This circle empowers you to develop leadership skills, mentor team members, and contribute to organizational success. Examples include setting goals, delegating tasks, and leading others within your professional sphere.

Self-Assessment Questions:
How important is taking on managerial responsibilities and leadership roles to guide teams and projects to success to you? (1-10)

How satisfied are you with your current level of engagement in managerial responsibilities and leadership roles? (1-10)

Tips and Ideas:
Develop leadership skills through workshops, courses, and mentorship programs.

Set clear organizational goals and create actionable plans to achieve them.

Delegate tasks effectively to team members based on their strengths and skills.

Provide mentorship and guidance to team members to foster professional growth.

Continuously evaluate and improve your leadership style and management practices.

Chapter 7: Mentoring and Coaching

Description: Mentoring and Coaching involve guiding and supporting others to achieve their goals and personal growth. This circle empowers you to share your expertise, offer guidance, and help individuals reach their full potential. Examples include providing coaching sessions, offering mentorship programs, and creating mentorship resources.

Self-Assessment Questions:

How important is guiding and supporting others through mentoring and coaching to you as a way of making a positive impact? (1-10)

How satisfied are you with your current level of involvement in mentoring and coaching activities? (1-10)

Tips and Ideas:

Offer mentorship programs or coaching sessions to individuals seeking guidance.

Share your expertise, insights, and experiences to help mentees overcome challenges.

Create mentorship resources, such as guides or workshops, to reach a wider audience.

Foster a supportive and growth-oriented environment for mentees to thrive.

Continuously develop your mentoring and coaching skills through learning and feedback.

Chapter 8: Artisanal Creations and Craftsmanship

Description: Artisanal Creations and Craftsmanship involve the art of crafting unique, handcrafted items that reflect your creativity and skills. This circle encourages you to explore traditional crafts and embrace the satisfaction of creating tangible works of art. Examples include woodworking, pottery, and handmade jewelry.

Self-Assessment Questions:

How important is expressing your creativity through artisanal creations and craftsmanship to you? (1-10)

How satisfied are you with your current level of involvement in crafting and artisanal projects? (1-10)

Tips and Ideas:

Learn traditional crafting techniques, such as woodworking, weaving, or ceramics.

Create a small home studio where you can dedicate time to your craft.

Host workshops or classes to teach others your crafting skills and techniques.

Sell your handmade creations through local markets, online platforms, or craft fairs.

Collaborate with other artisans to create unique and innovative cross-craft projects.

Chapter 9: Culinary Arts and Gastronomy

Description: Culinary Arts and Gastronomy revolve around the pleasures of cooking, experimenting with flavors, and creating delightful culinary experiences. This circle invites you to explore diverse cuisines, refine your cooking skills, and appreciate the art of food preparation. Examples include trying new recipes, hosting themed dinner parties, and experimenting with molecular gastronomy.

Self-Assessment Questions:

How important is cooking, culinary exploration, and sharing food experiences to you? (1-10)

How satisfied are you with your current culinary skills and culinary journey? (1-10)

Tips and Ideas:

Experiment with different cooking styles, ingredients, and cuisines.

Attend cooking classes or workshops to enhance your culinary techniques.

Create a food blog or social media account to document your culinary creations.

Host themed dinners or potlucks to share your love of cooking with friends and family.

Explore sustainable and locally-sourced ingredients to align with ethical culinary practices.

Chapter 10: Art and Museums

Description: Art and Museums encompass the exploration of creative expressions and artistic creations in various forms. Whether you're a painter, sculptor, or digital artist, this circle invites you to dive into your imagination. Examples include painting vibrant landscapes, sculpting intricate figurines, and creating digital illustrations.

Self-Assessment Questions:

How important is expressing yourself through art and exploring creative avenues to you? (1-10)

How satisfied are you with your current artistic endeavors and creative exploration? (1-10)

Tips and Ideas:

Dedicate regular time to create art, allowing your creativity to flow naturally.

Visit art galleries and museums to find inspiration and connect with other artists.

Collaborate with fellow artists on joint projects to learn and grow together.

Share your artwork online through social media platforms and art communities.

Consider offering art workshops to share your skills and passion with others.

Chapter 11: Designing and Building Things

Description: Designing and Building Things is about creating, designing, and constructing objects and structures that embody your creative vision. This circle empowers you to bring your ideas to life through innovative design and hands-on craftsmanship. Examples include designing furniture, building architectural models, and constructing DIY projects.

Self-Assessment Questions:
How important is expressing your creativity through design and hands-on building to you? (1-10)

How satisfied are you with your current level of involvement in designing and building projects? (1-10)

Tips and Ideas:
Learn design software and tools to visualize your ideas effectively.

Start small with DIY projects to develop your building and construction skills.

Collaborate with architects and engineers to bring architectural designs to fruition.

Enter design competitions to challenge your creativity and gain recognition.

Create a portfolio showcasing your design and building projects for potential clients or employers.

Chapter 12: Online Digital and Influence

Description: Online Digital and Influence revolves around building a meaningful online presence, creating digital content, and connecting with a global audience. This circle empowers you to share your ideas, insights, and creativity with others through various digital platforms. Examples include starting a blog, hosting webinars, and collaborating with fellow online influencers.

Self-Assessment Questions:

How important is building a digital presence and connecting with a global audience through online platforms to you? (1-10)

How satisfied are you with your current level of online influence and digital content creation? (1-10)

Tips and Ideas:

Choose a niche or topic that resonates with your interests and expertise.

Consistently create valuable and engaging content to attract and retain followers.

Collaborate with other online influencers to expand your reach and impact.

Engage with your audience through interactive content, polls, and Q&A sessions.

Experiment with different digital formats, such as videos, podcasts, or written articles, to diversify your content.

Chapter 13: Teaching and Educational Advocacy

Description: Teaching and Educational Advocacy involve promoting education reform, mentoring, and empowering learners to reach their full potential. This circle empowers you to make a lasting impact on education by advocating for inclusive learning environments and sharing your knowledge with others. Examples include advocating for inclusive curricula, mentoring students, and organizing educational workshops.

Self-Assessment Questions:
How important is promoting education and empowering learners through education and teaching to you? (1-10)

How satisfied are you with your current level of involvement in teaching and educational advocacy activities? (1-10)

Tips and Ideas:
Advocate for inclusive education policies and support marginalized learners.

Mentor students or aspiring professionals in your field to guide their growth.

Create educational resources, such as lesson plans or online courses, to share your expertise.

Organize workshops or webinars on educational topics to engage a broader audience.

Collaborate with educators and experts to develop innovative teaching methods and curricula.

Chapter 14: Educational Research and Innovation

Description: Educational Research and Innovation involve exploring new learning techniques, developing innovative curricula, and advancing the field of education. This circle empowers you to contribute to the improvement of educational practices and create meaningful learning experiences. Examples include conducting research on effective teaching methods, designing educational apps, and publishing educational papers.

Self-Assessment Questions:
How important is engaging in educational research and innovation to improve learning outcomes to you? (1-10)

How satisfied are you with your current level of involvement in educational research and innovation? (1-10)

Tips and Ideas:
Study emerging trends in education and identify areas for research and improvement.

Collaborate with educators and researchers to design and conduct educational studies.

Develop innovative curricula or learning materials to address specific learning needs.

Publish educational research findings in academic journals or present them at conferences.

Create educational apps, tools, or platforms that enhance learning experiences for students.

Chapter 15: Elderly Care and Aging Advocacy

Description: Elderly Care and Aging Advocacy involve supporting and advocating for the well-being of the elderly population. This circle empowers you to provide companionship, organize activities, and advocate for policies that enhance the quality of life for seniors. Examples include volunteering at senior centers, providing companionship to older adults, and advocating for senior rights.

Self-Assessment Questions:

How important is advocating for the well-being of the elderly and contributing to their quality of life to you? (1-10)

How satisfied are you with your current level of involvement in elderly care and aging advocacy? (1-10)

Tips and Ideas:

Volunteer at senior centers or retirement homes to engage with older adults.

Offer companionship and support to seniors in your community who may be isolated.

Organize recreational activities, workshops, or events that cater to the elderly population.

Advocate for policies that address the needs and rights of seniors in your local area.

Collaborate with geriatric professionals and organizations to promote healthy aging.

Chapter 16: Nature and Environmental Stewardship

Description: Nature and Environmental Stewardship involve caring for and preserving the natural world while promoting sustainable practices. This circle empowers you to participate in reforestation projects, organize eco-friendly events, and educate others about conservation. Examples include practicing zero-waste living, advocating for sustainable practices, and engaging in environmental activism.

Self-Assessment Questions:

How important is contributing to the preservation of the environment and promoting sustainable practices to you? (1-10)

How satisfied are you with your current level of involvement in nature and environmental stewardship activities? (1-10)

Tips and Ideas:

Participate in reforestation projects or tree-planting initiatives to support ecosystem health.

Organize eco-friendly events, workshops, or clean-up activities in your community.

Educate others about conservation and sustainable practices through awareness campaigns.

Advocate for policies and initiatives that promote environmental protection and sustainability.

Adopt a zero-waste lifestyle by reducing consumption, recycling, and minimizing environmental impact.

Chapter 17: Environmental Activism and Conservation

Description: Environmental Activism and Conservation focus on protecting and preserving the environment and natural resources. This circle empowers you to take action against climate change, promote sustainable practices, and raise awareness about environmental issues. Examples include participating in clean-up events, advocating for renewable energy, and supporting conservation initiatives.

Self-Assessment Questions:

How important is advocating for environmental protection and contributing to conservation efforts to you? (1-10)

How satisfied are you with your current level of involvement in environmental activism and conservation? (1-10)

Tips and Ideas:

Join environmental organizations and volunteer for clean-up and restoration projects.

Advocate for policies that promote renewable energy, reduce pollution, and protect natural habitats.

Raise awareness about environmental issues through social media, educational workshops, and public talks.

Support sustainable practices in your daily life, such as reducing waste and using eco-friendly products.

Collaborate with researchers, scientists, and policymakers to advance environmental protection efforts.

Chapter 18: Cybersecurity and Digital Privacy

Description: Cybersecurity and Digital Privacy focus on ensuring online safety and privacy through proactive cybersecurity measures. This circle empowers you to protect yourself and others from digital threats and raise awareness about digital security best practices. Examples include learning encryption methods, promoting safe online behavior, and participating in cybersecurity forums.

Self-Assessment Questions:
How important is cybersecurity and safeguarding digital privacy in today's interconnected world to you? (1-10)

How satisfied are you with your current level of knowledge and efforts in cybersecurity? (1-10)

Tips and Ideas:
Learn cybersecurity basics, including password management and data encryption.

Share online safety tips and resources with friends, family, and your community.

Participate in cybersecurity workshops and forums to stay updated on emerging threats.

Offer cybersecurity consultations or workshops to educate others about online risks.

Collaborate with cybersecurity experts to develop educational materials and resources.

Chapter 19: Astronomy and Space Exploration

Description: Astronomy and Space Exploration involves gazing into the mysteries of the universe, studying celestial bodies, and space research. This circle empowers you to study space-related fields, join space organizations and deepen your understanding of the cosmos. Examples include observing celestial events, joining astronomy clubs, and studying space-related fields.

Self-Assessment Questions:

How important is exploring the wonders of astronomy and space exploration to you as a means of expanding your perspective? (1-10)

How satisfied are you with your current level of involvement in astronomy and space exploration? (1-10)

Tips and Ideas:

Join astronomy clubs or online communities to connect with fellow space enthusiasts.

Observe celestial events such as meteor showers, eclipses, and planetary alignments.

Study astronomy online or take courses to deepen your knowledge of space-related topics.

Contribute to citizen science projects by analyzing astronomical data and observations.

Support space research and advocacy organizations to contribute to advancements in space exploration.

Chapter 20: Movie Watching and Appreciation

Description: Immerse yourself in the world of movies or series, exploring diverse genres, and cinematic experiences that transport you to different realms of imagination. Examples include classic movies from different eras, understanding their cultural and historical significance, exploring various genres, from drama and comedy to science fiction and animation.

Self-Assessment Questions:

How important is the act of movie watching and appreciating movies to you?

How satisfied are you with your current engagement in the world of movies?

Tips and Ideas:

Create a home theater environment that enhances your movie-watching experience.

Study film theory and storytelling techniques to deepen your understanding.

Keep a film journal to document your thoughts and reflections on different movies.

Engage in discussions and debates with fellow movie enthusiasts to gain new perspectives.

Attend film festivals, screenings, and cinema clubs to connect with others who share your passion.

Chapter 21: Cinematic and Film Creation

Description: Cinematic and Film Creation involve producing, directing, or participating in film and cinematic projects to tell captivating stories. This circle empowers you to harness the power of visual storytelling and bring narratives to life through the art of filmmaking. Examples include writing scripts, collaborating with film crews, and participating in cinema and films projects.

Self-Assessment Questions:
How important is using the medium of film to tell stories and express creativity to you? (1-10)

How satisfied are you with your current involvement in film and cinematic projects? (1-10)

Tips and Ideas:
Learn scriptwriting techniques and develop engaging and compelling storylines.

Collaborate with a team of filmmakers to bring your vision to the screen.

Study film production and editing to enhance your technical skills.

Submit your work to film festivals or online platforms to showcase your talent.

Experiment with various film genres and styles to broaden your creative horizons.

Chapter 22: Financial Stability and Prosperity

Description: Financial Stability and Prosperity involve achieving financial security and effectively managing your resources. This circle empowers you to make informed financial decisions, invest wisely, and work toward achieving your financial goals. Examples include creating a budget, seeking financial advice, and exploring investment opportunities.

Self-Assessment Questions:

How important is achieving financial stability and managing your resources responsibly to you? (1-10)

How satisfied are you with your current level of financial stability and financial management practices? (1-10)

Tips and Ideas:

Create a detailed budget to track your income, expenses, and savings goals.

Invest in financial education to enhance your understanding of personal finance and investments.

Seek advice from financial advisors to develop a strategic financial plan.

Explore different investment opportunities, such as stocks, real estate, or mutual funds.

Practice disciplined saving and spending habits to achieve your long-term financial objectives.

Chapter 23: Family Bonds and Relationships

Description: Family Bonds and Relationships involve nurturing and fostering strong relationships within the family unit (includes relationships you consider close enough to be as family). This circle empowers you to create lasting connections, foster open communication, and build cherished memories with your loved ones. Examples include organizing family gatherings, fostering sibling relationships, and participating in family traditions.

Self-Assessment Questions:

How important is nurturing and strengthening family bonds to you as a source of emotional support and belonging? (1-10)

How satisfied are you with the quality of your current family relationships and connections? (1-10)

Tips and Ideas:

Spend quality time with family members through regular family outings or dinners.

Initiate open and honest communication to build trust and understanding among family members.

Create and uphold family traditions that hold special meaning and significance.

Plan collaborative projects or activities that involve multiple generations of your family.

Offer support and be there for each other during significant life events and challenges.

Chapter 24: Friendship and Camaraderie

Description: Friendship and Camaraderie revolve around cultivating and cherishing deep connections with friends. This circle empowers you to create meaningful relationships, provide support, and foster a sense of belonging within your social circle. Examples include organizing social gatherings, communicating regularly with friends, and establishing friendship rituals.

Self-Assessment Questions:

How important is cultivating strong friendships and fostering a sense of camaraderie to you? (1-10)

How satisfied are you with the quality of your current friendships and social connections? (1-10)

Tips and Ideas:

Initiate social gatherings or events to strengthen your bonds with friends.

Be a supportive and reliable friend by actively listening and offering assistance.

Create rituals or traditions that bring you and your friends together on a regular basis.

Communicate regularly through various channels, such as texts, calls, or social media.

Engage in shared activities or hobbies that deepen your connection and provide shared experiences.

Chapter 25: Romance and Romantic Partnerships

Description: Romance and Romantic Partnerships involve nurturing and cherishing intimate relationships and finding love and companionship. This circle empowers you to plan romantic dates, communicate openly, express affection, and create lasting memories. Examples include building emotional connections, fostering romantic gestures, and maintaining healthy partnerships.

Self-Assessment Questions:

How important is nurturing and cherishing romantic relationships and finding love and companionship to you? (1-10)

How satisfied are you with your current level of engagement in romance and romantic partnership activities? (1-10)

Tips and Ideas:

Plan romantic dates, surprise getaways, or special evenings to cultivate intimacy.

Communicate openly and honestly with your partner to build trust and understanding.

Express affection through meaningful gestures, love letters, or acts of kindness.

Create lasting memories by sharing experiences, traditions, and memorable moments.

Prioritize self-care and personal growth to enhance your own well-being within relationships.

Chapter 26: Music Creation, Production and Expression

Description: Music Creation and Production involve finding purpose through creating, performing, or producing music. This circle empowers you to learn to play an instrument, compose music, and engage in musical performances that resonate with your emotions and creativity. Examples include joining a band, hosting music events, and composing or producing music.

Self-Assessment Questions:

How important is music as a means of expressing emotions, creativity, and connecting with others to you? (1-10)

How satisfied are you with your current level of music creation, production and expression? (1-10)

Tips and Ideas:

Learn to play a musical instrument that resonates with your interests and passions.

Explore different musical genres and styles to expand your musical horizons.

Write and compose your music to express your thoughts, emotions, and experiences.

Collaborate with fellow musicians or join a band to create and produce musical arrangements.

Share your music through performances, open mics, or online platforms to connect with an audience.

Chapter 27: Music Appreciation and Enjoyment

Description: Delve into the world of music, exploring different genres, instruments, and rhythms that resonate with your emotions and uplift your spirit. Examples include discovering compositions, exploring contemporary music genres, from rock and pop to electronic and hip-hop.

Self-Assessment Questions:

How important is music appreciation and enjoyment in your life?

How satisfied are you with your current level of engagement with music?

Tips and Ideas:

Attend live music performances to experience the magic of music in person.

Create curated playlists that match different moods and occasions.

Design and set up your own sound system.

Explore music history and cultural influences to gain a deeper understanding of different genres.

Join music communities, attend jam sessions, and collaborate with fellow music enthusiasts.

Chapter 28: Healing and Holistic Practices

Description: Healing and Holistic Practices involve embracing techniques such as yoga, meditation, and alternative therapies for overall well-being. This circle empowers you to cultivate mindfulness, reduce stress, and promote holistic wellness in both yourself and others. Examples include practicing meditation, learning holistic healing techniques, and organizing wellness retreats.

Self-Assessment Questions:

How important is cultivating holistic well-being and embracing healing practices for your overall health and balance? (1-10)

How satisfied are you with your current level of engagement in healing and holistic practices? (1-10)

Tips and Ideas:

Establish a regular mindfulness practice to enhance self-awareness and reduce stress.

Learn and practice holistic healing techniques, such as acupuncture or aromatherapy.

Become a certified instructor in practices like yoga, meditation, or Reiki to guide others.

Organize wellness retreats or workshops to share holistic practices with a wider audience.

Incorporate healing rituals and practices into your daily routine to promote inner balance.

Chapter 29: Health and Medicine

Description: Health and Medicine involve serving others through medical, nursing, or other healthcare-related roles. This circle empowers you to contribute to the well-being of individuals and communities through medical education, volunteering, and health-related initiatives. Examples include pursuing medical education, offering health education workshops, and participating in medical missions.

Self-Assessment Questions:
How important is serving others through healthcare-related roles and contributing to public health to you? (1-10)

How satisfied are you with your current level of involvement in health and medicine-related activities? (1-10)

Tips and Ideas:
Pursue a medical education or training to become a healthcare professional.

Volunteer at clinics, hospitals, or medical outreach programs to support underserved populations.

Offer health education workshops or seminars to empower individuals to make informed choices.

Participate in medical missions or humanitarian trips to provide medical care to those in need.

Collaborate with local health organizations to promote preventive care and wellness initiatives.

Chapter 30: Historical Exploration

Description: Historical Exploration involves delving into history and cultural heritage to gain insights into past societies and traditions. This circle empowers you to connect with the past, explore historical records, and contribute to preserving cultural heritage. Examples include visiting historical sites, engaging in genealogy research, and writing historical articles.

Self-Assessment Questions:

How important is exploring history and cultural heritage to gain a deeper understanding of human societies to you? (1-10)

How satisfied are you with your current level of historical exploration and engagement? (1-10)

Tips and Ideas:

Visit historical sites, museums, and archives to immerse yourself in different historical periods.

Study historical records, documents, and artifacts to piece together narratives of the past.

Engage in genealogy research to trace your own family history and heritage.

Write historical articles, essays, or books to share your discoveries and insights.

Participate in historical reenactments or events to experience and recreate moments from the past.

Chapter 31: Fun, Humor and Joyful Engagement

Description: Fun, Humor and Joyful Engagement involve spreading laughter and positivity through humor and lighthearted interactions. This circle empowers you to develop comedic skills, bring joy to others, and create moments of levity in everyday life. Examples include improving comedic abilities, performing stand-up comedy, and organizing comedy events.

Self-Assessment Questions:
How important is using humor to bring joy, laughter, and positivity to your interactions and surroundings? (1-10)

How satisfied are you with your current level of engagement in fun, humor and joyful engagement activities? (1-10)

Tips and Ideas:
Develop your comedic skills through improv classes, joke writing, and comedic timing practice.

Perform stand-up comedy at open mic nights or comedy clubs to share your humor with an audience.

Create funny content, memes, or videos to spread laughter through social media.

Organize or participate in comedy events, showcases, or workshops in your community.

Use humor as a tool to diffuse tense situations, build connections, and bring joy to others.

Chapter 32: Innovation in Technology and Science

Description: Innovation in Technology and Science involves pioneering advancements in technological and scientific fields. This circle empowers you to contribute to groundbreaking discoveries, engage in research, and develop innovative solutions to complex challenges. Examples include participating in hackathons, contributing to scientific research, and inventing new technologies.

Self-Assessment Questions:
How important is contributing to technological and scientific advancements and driving innovation in your chosen field to you? (1-10)

How satisfied are you with your current level of involvement in technology and science innovation? (1-10)

Tips and Ideas:
Collaborate on technology projects, hackathons, or coding challenges to hone your skills.

Participate in scientific research projects or studies to contribute to new knowledge.

Innovate by developing new technologies, software, or applications that address real-world problems.

Attend conferences, seminars, or workshops to stay updated on the latest advancements in your field.

Mentor aspiring innovators and share your knowledge to foster a culture of continuous discovery.

Chapter 33: Language Preservation and Revitalization

Description: Language Preservation and Revitalization involve preserving and reviving endangered languages to ensure cultural heritage and diversity. This circle empowers you to learn and teach languages, collaborate with linguists, and engage in language workshops. Examples include learning endangered languages, organizing language revitalization efforts, and creating language resources.

Self-Assessment Questions:

How important is preserving and revitalizing endangered languages to you as a means of honoring cultural heritage and promoting linguistic diversity? (1-10)

How satisfied are you with your current involvement in language preservation and revitalization activities? (1-10)

Tips and Ideas:

Learn and become proficient in endangered languages to contribute to their preservation.

Collaborate with linguists, language experts, and cultural organizations to support revitalization efforts.

Organize language workshops, classes, or immersion programs to teach others the endangered language.

Create language learning resources, books, or digital content to make the language accessible.

Advocate for the recognition and inclusion of endangered languages in educational and cultural programs.

Chapter 34: Language Study and Communication

Description: Language Study and Communication involve mastering languages and effective communication to connect with diverse individuals. This circle empowers you to learn new languages, practice public speaking, and engage in bilingual communication. Examples include learning multiple languages, offering language tutoring, and writing bilingual content.

Self-Assessment Questions:

How important is mastering languages and effective communication to connect with people from different cultures and backgrounds to you? (1-10)

How satisfied are you with your current level of language proficiency and communication skills? (1-10)

Tips and Ideas:

Learn new languages through courses, apps, or immersion programs to expand your linguistic abilities.

Practice public speaking by joining speaking clubs, giving presentations, or participating in debates.

Write bilingual content, articles, or blogs to engage with a wider audience.

Offer language tutoring or teaching services to help others learn and improve their language skills.

Engage in cross-cultural conversations and exchange experiences with individuals from diverse linguistic backgrounds.

Chapter 35: Coding and Programming

Description: Coding and Programming involve engaging in software development and coding projects. This circle invites you to harness the power of technology to create innovative solutions and applications. Examples include developing mobile apps, coding interactive websites, and contributing to open-source projects.

Self-Assessment Questions:

How important is coding and programming as a means of creative expression and problem-solving for you? (1-10)

How satisfied are you with your current coding skills and level of involvement in programming projects? (1-10)

Tips and Ideas:

Learn coding languages that align with your interests and project goals.

Work on personal coding projects to apply and enhance your skills.

Collaborate with other programmers on open-source initiatives to contribute to the community.

Attend coding workshops and online courses to stay updated on the latest technologies.

Build a coding portfolio showcasing your projects and accomplishments to potential employers.

Chapter 36: Animal Companionship and Care

Description: This circle centers on nurturing strong bonds with animals and supporting their well-being. It involves adopting pets, volunteering at animal shelters, and participating in conservation efforts. Examples include adopting a rescue dog, volunteering at a wildlife sanctuary, and promoting responsible pet ownership.

Self-Assessment Questions:
How important is caring for and advocating for animal welfare to you? (1-10)

How satisfied are you with your current level of involvement in animal companionship and care activities? (1-10)

Tips and Ideas:
Adopt a pet from a shelter or rescue organization to provide a loving home.

Volunteer at animal shelters to assist with daily care and adoption events.

Support animal conservation efforts by donating to wildlife preservation organizations.

Organize awareness campaigns to raise funds and awareness for endangered species.

Educate your community about responsible pet ownership and the importance of spaying/neutering.

Chapter 37: Emotional and Mental Well-being

Description: Emotional and Mental Well-being involve promoting well-being and emotional health for individuals and communities. This circle empowers you to provide counseling services, lead well-being workshops, and create resources that support mental and emotional wellness. Examples include offering counseling sessions, leading mindfulness workshops, and raising awareness about mental health.

Self-Assessment Questions:

How important is promoting emotional and mental well-being and providing support for individuals' emotional health to you? (1-10)

How satisfied are you with your current level of involvement in emotional and mental well-being activities? (1-10)

Tips and Ideas:

Offer counseling or therapy services to individuals seeking support for mental and emotional well-being.

Lead well-being workshops or seminars on topics such as stress management, mindfulness, or resilience.

Create mental health resources, such as self-help guides or online content, to reach a broader audience.

Raise awareness about mental health issues and reduce stigma through advocacy and education.

Collaborate with mental health professionals and organizations to provide comprehensive support.

Chapter 38: Well-being Mindfulness Coaching

Description: Well-being Mindfulness Coaching involve teaching mindfulness practices and coaching individuals toward holistic well-being. This circle empowers you to become a certified mindfulness coach, offer meditation classes, and lead wellness retreats. Examples include practicing mindfulness, learning coaching techniques, and creating well-being resources.

Self-Assessment Questions:

How important is promoting mindfulness and holistic well-being through coaching and teaching to you? (1-10)

How satisfied are you with your current level of engagement in mindfulness and well-being coaching activities? (1-10)

Tips and Ideas:

Become a certified mindfulness coach or instructor through training programs.

Offer meditation classes, workshops, or guided sessions to help individuals cultivate mindfulness.

Create well-being podcasts, videos, or online courses to reach a wider audience.

Lead wellness retreats that provide participants with opportunities for self-discovery and relaxation.

Continuously deepen your understanding of mindfulness practices and coaching techniques.

Chapter 39: Entrepreneurship and Innovative Ventures

Description: Entrepreneurship and Innovative Ventures involve creating, launching, and growing new businesses, products, or ideas. This circle empowers you to identify market gaps, innovate products/services, and contribute to economic growth. Examples include starting a tech startup, launching a sustainable fashion brand, and developing innovative solutions to societal challenges.

Self-Assessment Questions:
How important is entrepreneurship and creating innovative ventures to you as a means of making a meaningful impact? (1-10)

How satisfied are you with your current level of involvement in entrepreneurial endeavors? (1-10)

Tips and Ideas:
Identify problems or opportunities in your chosen industry and brainstorm innovative solutions.

Develop a comprehensive business plan outlining your goals, target market, and strategies.

Seek funding through grants, angel investors, venture capital, or crowdfunding platforms.

Collaborate with mentors, advisors, and fellow entrepreneurs to gain insights and guidance.

Embrace a growth mindset and continuously adapt your business model based on feedback and market trends.

Chapter 40: Outdoor Adventures and Exploration

Description: Outdoor Adventures and Exploration involve engaging in outdoor activities, sports, and adventures that challenge and invigorate the body. This circle empowers you to try new outdoor sports, go on hiking expeditions, and participate in adventure races. Examples include rock climbing, camping trips, and exploring natural landscapes.

Self-Assessment Questions:

How important is seeking adventure and engaging in outdoor activities to challenge yourself and connect with nature to you? (1-10)

How satisfied are you with your current level of engagement in outdoor adventures and exploration? (1-10)

Tips and Ideas:

Try new outdoor sports or activities, such as kayaking, mountain biking, or surfing.

Plan hiking expeditions to explore natural landscapes, trails, and scenic areas.

Organize camping trips or backpacking adventures to experience the beauty of the outdoors.

Participate in adventure races, obstacle courses, or endurance events to test your limits.

Connect with outdoor communities, clubs, or groups to share experiences and plan adventures.

Chapter 41: Parenting and Caregiving

Description: Parenting and Caregiving involve nurturing and raising children and providing care and support to loved ones. This circle empowers you to create a supportive home environment, organize family activities, and offer caregiving resources. Examples include attending parenting classes, fostering family bonds, and providing care for elderly family members.

Self-Assessment Questions:

How important is nurturing and providing care and support to your family members and loved ones to you? (1-10)

How satisfied are you with your current level of engagement in parenting and caregiving responsibilities? (1-10)

Tips and Ideas:

Attend parenting classes or workshops to enhance your parenting skills and knowledge.

Create a supportive and nurturing home environment that fosters healthy family dynamics.

Organize family activities, outings, and traditions to strengthen family bonds.

Offer caregiving resources, support groups, or workshops for caregivers in your community.

Balance your own well-being while caring for others by seeking self-care and support.

Chapter 42: Creative Pursuits (General)

Description: Creative Pursuits (General) involve engaging in hobbies and creative activities that ignite personal passions. This circle empowers you to explore new hobbies, join creative clubs, and dedicate time to creative projects. Examples include experimenting with art, joining writing groups, and immersing yourself in creative expression.

Self-Assessment Questions:

How important is dedicating time to creative pursuits that bring you joy and fulfillment to you? (1-10)

How satisfied are you with your current level of engagement in creative activities? (1-10)

Tips and Ideas:

Explore new hobbies and activities that align with your interests and passions.

Join creative clubs, writing groups, or art communities to connect with like-minded individuals.

Dedicate regular time to creative projects, whether it's painting, writing, crafting, or playing music.

Share your creative work with others through exhibitions, showcases, or online platforms.

Embrace the process of exploration and experimentation as you pursue your creative passions.

Chapter 43: Philanthropy and Giving Back

Description: Philanthropy and Giving Back involve contributing time, resources, and effort to support charitable causes. This circle empowers you to donate to NGOs, volunteer at shelters, organize charity events, and create fundraising campaigns. Examples include participating in community service, advocating for social change, and making a positive impact.

Self-Assessment Questions:

How important is giving back to your community and making a positive impact through philanthropic efforts to you? (1-10)

How satisfied are you with your current level of involvement in philanthropy and giving back activities? (1-10)

Tips and Ideas:

Donate to NGOs, charitable organizations, or causes that resonate with your values.

Volunteer your time at local shelters, food banks, or community service projects.

Organize charity events, fundraisers, or donation drives to raise awareness and support.

Advocate for social change and raise awareness about issues that matter to you.

Collaborate with others to amplify the impact of your philanthropic efforts and create lasting change.

Chapter 44: Political Engagement and Civic Participation

Description: Political Engagement and Civic Participation involve taking an active role in politics and civic activities to influence positive change. This circle empowers you to attend town hall meetings, join political campaigns, advocate for policy changes, and participate in the democratic process. Examples include voting in elections, organizing community initiatives, and engaging in civil discourse.

Self-Assessment Questions:
How important is being actively engaged in politics and civic activities to advocate for positive change in your community and society? (1-10)

How satisfied are you with your current level of involvement in political engagement and civic participation? (1-10)

Tips and Ideas:
Attend town hall meetings, community forums, and public discussions to stay informed about local issues.

Join political campaigns, volunteer for candidates, or participate in grassroots organizing.

Vote in elections and encourage others to exercise their right to vote through voter registration efforts.

Advocate for policy changes by contacting your representatives, writing op-eds, and participating in advocacy campaigns.

Engage in civil discourse and discussions to better understand diverse perspectives and contribute to informed decision-making.

Chapter 45: Public Speaking and Motivation

Description: Public Speaking and Motivation involve inspiring and motivating others through effective public speaking and coaching techniques. This circle empowers you to improve public speaking skills, offer motivational talks, create online courses, and lead personal development workshops. Examples include delivering impactful speeches, leading motivational sessions, and empowering others to achieve their goals.

Self-Assessment Questions:

How important is inspiring and motivating others through public speaking and coaching to you as a way to make a positive impact? (1-10)

How satisfied are you with your current level of engagement in public speaking and motivational coaching activities? (1-10)

Tips and Ideas:

Improve public speaking skills through practice, speech coaching, and presentation training.

Offer motivational talks or keynote speeches at events, conferences, or workshops.

Create online courses or workshops on personal development, goal-setting, and self-improvement.

Lead personal development workshops that empower participants to overcome challenges and achieve success.

Share personal stories of triumph and growth to inspire and connect with your audience.

Chapter 46: Quantitative Analysis and Insight

Description: Quantitative Analysis and Insight involve analyzing data and statistics to gain insights and inform decision-making. This circle empowers you to learn data analysis tools, contribute to research studies, and offer data analysis services. Examples include conducting market research, performing data-driven analysis, and interpreting statistical trends.

Self-Assessment Questions:

How important is using data analysis and quantitative insights to inform decision-making and drive meaningful change to you? (1-10)

How satisfied are you with your current level of engagement in quantitative analysis and insight activities? (1-10)

Tips and Ideas:

Learn data analysis tools and software to effectively analyze and interpret data sets.

Contribute to research studies, surveys, or data-driven projects in your field of interest.

Offer data analysis services to organizations, businesses, or researchers seeking insights.

Collaborate with experts to interpret statistical trends and present data-driven findings.

Apply quantitative analysis to identify patterns, trends, and opportunities for informed decision-making.

Chapter 47: Qualitative Exploration and Discovery

Description: Qualitative Exploration and Discovery involve conducting in-depth research and qualitative analysis to uncover insights and narratives. This circle empowers you to conduct interviews, gather qualitative data, analyze narratives, and contribute to ethnographic studies. Examples include conducting qualitative research projects, exploring human experiences, and uncovering hidden stories.

Self-Assessment Questions:
How important is conducting qualitative research and uncovering deeper insights into human experiences and narratives to you? (1-10)

How satisfied are you with your current level of engagement in qualitative exploration and discovery activities? (1-10)

Tips and Ideas:
Conduct interviews and gather qualitative data to explore human perspectives and stories.

Analyze narratives, stories, or case studies to uncover underlying themes and insights.

Contribute to ethnographic studies that provide a rich understanding of cultures and societies.

Collaborate with researchers, anthropologists, or sociologists to deepen qualitative research.

Use qualitative insights to inform social initiatives, policy recommendations, or storytelling projects.

Chapter 48: Artificial Intelligence and Ethics

Description: Artificial Intelligence and Ethics involve exploring the ethical implications of AI and promoting responsible AI development. This circle delves into the potential risks and benefits of AI technologies. Examples include discussing the impact of AI on job displacement and advocating for transparent algorithms.

Self-Assessment Questions:

How important is understanding AI ethics and promoting responsible AI development to you? (1-10)

How satisfied are you with your current level of engagement in AI ethics discussions? (1-10)

Tips and Ideas:

Study AI ethics principles and guidelines to become well-versed in the subject.

Engage in online forums and discussions about AI's ethical challenges and solutions.

Contribute to the development of AI policy frameworks by sharing your insights.

Mentor AI developers and students to promote ethical considerations in their work.

Organize workshops and webinars on the ethical implications of emerging AI technologies.

Chapter 49: Personal-Development and Lifelong Learning

Description: Personal-Development and Lifelong Learning involve continuously improving personal skills, knowledge, and self-awareness. This circle empowers you to set learning goals, read diverse books, attend workshops, and practice self-reflection. Examples include pursuing personal growth, acquiring new skills, and expanding your intellectual horizons.

Self-Assessment Questions:
How important is investing in personal-development and lifelong learning to continuously improve and grow as an individual? (1-10)

How satisfied are you with your current level of engagement in personal-development and lifelong learning activities? (1-10)

Tips and Ideas:
Set specific learning goals to guide your personal and professional growth.

Read diverse books, articles, and materials to expand your knowledge and perspectives.

Attend workshops, seminars, or online courses that align with your interests and goals.

Practice self-reflection through journaling, meditation, or mindfulness to enhance self-awareness.

Embrace a growth mindset and seek opportunities for continuous learning and self-improvement.

Chapter 50: Social Entrepreneurship

Description: Social Entrepreneurship involves creating and managing businesses that prioritize social and environmental impact. This circle empowers you to identify social issues, develop business plans, seek impact investors, and measure social outcomes. Examples include launching social enterprises, driving positive change, and aligning business with social responsibility.

Self-Assessment Questions:

How important is creating a business that generates both financial profit and positive social impact through social entrepreneurship to you? (1-10)

How satisfied are you with your current level of involvement in social entrepreneurship activities? (1-10)

Tips and Ideas:

Identify social or environmental issues that align with your business vision and mission.

Develop a comprehensive business plan that outlines your social impact goals and strategies.

Seek impact investors, grants, or funding opportunities that support social entrepreneurship.

Measure and track social outcomes, such as community benefits or environmental improvements.

Collaborate with like-minded entrepreneurs, organizations, and stakeholders to amplify your impact.

Chapter 51: Informative Social Media Activism and Awareness

Description: Informative Social Media Activism and Awareness involve raising awareness and driving change through social media platforms. This circle empowers you to share informative content, engage with followers, participate in online campaigns, and collaborate with influencers. Examples include advocating for social causes, mobilizing online communities, and leveraging the power of digital platforms for social change.

Self-Assessment Questions:

How important is using social media as a tool for raising awareness, activism, and driving positive change to you? (1-10)

How satisfied are you with your current level of engagement in informative social media activism and awareness activities? (1-10)

Tips and Ideas:

Share informative and impactful content on social media platforms to educate your audience.

Engage with followers by responding to comments, initiating discussions, and fostering a sense of community.

Participate in online campaigns, challenges, or movements that align with your values.

Collaborate with influencers, activists, or organizations to amplify the reach of your message.

Use social media analytics to measure the impact of your activism and refine your strategies.

Chapter 52: Philosophical Exploration

Description: Philosophical Exploration involve delving into profound philosophical questions and ethical principles that guide human actions. This circle empowers you to engage in thoughtful debates, expand your moral reasoning, and explore the foundations of ethical theories. Examples include studying ethical dilemmas, participating in philosophical discussions, and reflecting on personal values.

Self-Assessment Questions:
How important is exploring philosophical questions and principles as a means of personal growth and critical thinking to you? (1-10)

How satisfied are you with your current level of engagement in philosophical exploration? (1-10)

Tips and Ideas:
Study major ethical theories, such as utilitarianism, deontology, and virtue ethics.

Engage in philosophical discussions with peers, book clubs, or online forums.

Write reflective essays or articles on ethical dilemmas and moral decision-making.

Organize ethics discussion groups or seminars to foster thoughtful conversations.

Apply philosophical principles to real-life situations to enhance your ethical decision-making.

Chapter 53: Spiritual and Philosophical Alignment

Description: Spiritual and Philosophical Alignment involve aligning with personal spiritual beliefs and exploring philosophical questions. This circle empowers you to practice meditation, engage in spiritual discussions, attend religious gatherings, and study philosophical texts. Examples include deepening your spirituality, seeking existential insights, and fostering a sense of purpose through philosophical exploration.

Self-Assessment Questions:

How important is exploring spirituality and delving into philosophical questions to guide your beliefs and actions in life? (1-10)

How satisfied are you with your current level of engagement in spiritual and philosophical alignment activities? (1-10)

Tips and Ideas:

Practice meditation, prayer, or mindfulness to cultivate a deeper connection to your spirituality.

Engage in philosophical discussions, debates, or reading groups to explore existential questions.

Attend religious gatherings, ceremonies, or services that align with your spiritual beliefs.

Study philosophical texts, literature, or teachings that resonate with your quest for understanding.

Reflect on your beliefs, values, and experiences to align your spiritual and philosophical journey.

Chapter 54: Spiritual Leadership and Guidance

Description: Spiritual Leadership and Guidance involve providing counseling, leadership, and support in spiritual and religious contexts. This circle empowers you to train as a spiritual leader, offer spiritual counseling, lead meditation sessions, and organize religious events. Examples include guiding others on their spiritual journey, fostering a sense of community, and facilitating meaningful rituals.

Self-Assessment Questions:
How important is providing spiritual guidance, counseling, and leadership within a spiritual or religious community to you? (1-10)

How satisfied are you with your current level of involvement in spiritual leadership and guidance activities? (1-10)

Tips and Ideas:
Pursue training or education to become a certified spiritual leader, minister, or religious guide.

Offer spiritual counseling, guidance, and support to individuals seeking answers and direction.

Lead meditation, prayer, or mindfulness sessions to promote spiritual well-being and growth.

Organize religious events, retreats, or workshops that provide opportunities for reflection and connection.

Foster a sense of community within your spiritual or religious group through regular gatherings and shared rituals.

Chapter 55: Agriculture and Farming Sustainability

Description: Agriculture and Farming Sustainability involve engaging in environmentally friendly farming and sustainable agricultural practices. This circle empowers you to start organic farming, use permaculture techniques, promote local food systems, and educate about sustainable agriculture. Examples include cultivating nutritious crops, reducing environmental impact, and advocating for a resilient food system.

Self-Assessment Questions:
How important is practicing sustainable agriculture and contributing to a healthier and more environmentally conscious food system to you? (1-10)

How satisfied are you with your current level of engagement in sustainable agriculture and farming activities? (1-10)

Tips and Ideas:
Start an organic farm or garden that focuses on cultivating crops without synthetic chemicals.

Implement permaculture principles to design efficient and sustainable agricultural systems.

Promote local food systems by supporting farmers' markets, community-supported agriculture (CSA), and farm-to-table initiatives.

Educate others about sustainable farming practices, composting, and reducing food waste.

Explore innovative methods such as hydroponics, aquaponics, or vertical farming to maximize space and resources.

Chapter 56: Technology Ethics and Policy Advocacy

Description: Technology Ethics and Policy Advocacy involve advocating for ethical technology use and influencing policy decisions. This circle empowers you to join tech ethics organizations, participate in policy discussions, write op-eds, and organize tech ethics workshops. Examples include promoting responsible technology development, addressing digital rights, and shaping ethical guidelines.

Self-Assessment Questions:

How important is advocating for ethical technology use and influencing policy decisions related to technology to you? (1-10)

How satisfied are you with your current level of engagement in technology ethics and policy advocacy activities? (1-10)

Tips and Ideas:

Join tech ethics organizations, think tanks, or forums that focus on ethical technology development.

Participate in policy discussions, contribute to whitepapers, and provide input on technology regulations.

Write op-eds, articles, or blog posts to raise awareness about ethical tech issues and promote informed discourse.

Organize workshops, webinars, or panel discussions that explore the ethical implications of emerging technologies.

Collaborate with experts, policymakers, and stakeholders to shape responsible and ethical tech practices.

Chapter 57: Theater and Performance Arts

Description: Theater and Performance Arts involve expressing creativity and emotions through acting, theater, and performance. This circle empowers you to join theater groups, participate in drama productions, attend acting workshops, and write and perform monologues. Examples include storytelling through performance, exploring characters, and engaging audiences through artistic expression.

Self-Assessment Questions:

How important is expressing creativity and emotions through theater and performance arts to you? (1-10)

How satisfied are you with your current level of engagement in theater and performance arts activities? (1-10)

Tips and Ideas:

Join local theater groups, acting troupes, or drama clubs to collaborate with fellow performers.

Participate in drama productions, plays, or theatrical events to showcase your acting skills and creativity.

Attend acting workshops, improvisation classes, or voice training sessions to enhance your performance abilities.

Write and perform monologues or original scripts that resonate with personal themes or messages.

Experiment with various performance styles, genres, and characters to broaden your theatrical repertoire.

Chapter 58: Travel and New Experiences

Description: Travel and New Experiences involve exploring new places, cultures, and experiences to broaden horizons. This circle empowers you to plan cultural trips, engage in adventure travel, volunteer abroad, and document travel experiences. Examples include immersing yourself in different environments, embracing cultural diversity, and fostering personal growth through exploration.

Self-Assessment Questions:

How important is experiencing new cultures, places, and adventures to broaden your perspective and enrich your life? (1-10)

How satisfied are you with your current level of engagement in travel and new experiences? (1-10)

Tips and Ideas:

Plan cultural trips to immerse yourself in the traditions, cuisine, and daily life of different communities.

Embrace adventure travel by trying new outdoor activities, exploring remote locations, and pushing your limits.

Volunteer abroad to contribute to community projects, support local initiatives, and make a positive impact.

Document your travel experiences through journaling, photography, or travel blogs to capture memories and insights.

Embrace the mindset of a traveler and approach each new experience with curiosity, openness, and a willingness to learn.

Chapter 59: Urban Planning and Sustainable Cities

Description: Urban Planning and Sustainable Cities involve contributing to well-designed and sustainable urban environments. This circle empowers you to study urban planning, advocate for green spaces, participate in city planning projects, and promote eco-friendly infrastructure. Examples include designing livable cities, fostering community engagement, and advocating for sustainable urban development.

Self-Assessment Questions:
How important is contributing to the creation of well-designed, sustainable, and livable urban environments to you? (1-10)

How satisfied are you with your current level of engagement in urban planning and sustainable cities activities? (1-10)

Tips and Ideas:
Study urban planning, urban design, or architecture to gain a deeper understanding of sustainable city development.

Advocate for the creation and preservation of green spaces, parks, and public recreational areas.

Participate in city planning projects, community initiatives, and urban development discussions.

Promote eco-friendly infrastructure and initiatives such as bike lanes, renewable energy sources, and waste reduction programs.

Collaborate with city officials, urban designers, and community members to shape sustainable urban environments that prioritize people and the planet.

Chapter 60: Media and Video Creation

Description: Media and Video Creation involve producing video and media content to inform, entertain, and engage audiences. This circle empowers you to learn video editing, create vlogs, host webinars, and collaborate with other content creators. Examples include sharing stories through visual media, creating educational content, and leveraging digital platforms for creative expression.

Self-Assessment Questions:

How important is using video and media creation to communicate, entertain, and connect with audiences in the digital age? (1-10)

How satisfied are you with your current level of engagement in video and media creation activities? (1-10)

Tips and Ideas:

Learn video editing software and techniques to create polished and engaging video content.

Start a vlog or video series to share your experiences, insights, and stories with an online audience.

Host webinars, online workshops, or live streaming sessions to provide valuable information and engage with viewers in real time.

Collaborate with other content creators, artists, or experts to produce multimedia projects and cross-promote content.

Experiment with different video formats, styles, and platforms to find your unique voice and connect with your target audience.

Chapter 61: Drinking and Tasting Appreciation

Description: Indulge in the art of tasting and appreciating various beverages, from fine wines to exotic teas. Immerse yourself in the sensory experience and cultural significance of each sip. Examples include the world of red, white, and sparkling wines, learning about different grape varieties and regions. Understanding the rich flavors of single-origin coffee beans, experimenting with brewing methods.

Self-Assessment Questions:

How important is exploring and appreciating different beverages in your life?

How satisfied are you with your current level of knowledge and experience in this area?

Tips and Ideas:

Attend tasting events or workshops to expand your palate.

Explore local wineries, breweries, and tea houses.

Educate yourself about the production and history of your favorite beverages.

Keep a beverage journal to track your tasting experiences.

Experiment with food pairings to enhance the flavors of your drinks.

Chapter 62: Shopping Retail (Online or Physical)

Description: Discover the joy of shopping, not just as a transaction, but as an expression of personal style. Explore fashion, groceries, home decor, and more to curate a unique and reflective lifestyle. Examples include exploring thrift stores and vintage shops, supermarket exploration, online shopping and browsing.

Self-Assessment Questions:

How important is shopping and curating your personal style in your life?

How satisfied are you with your current shopping experiences and choices?

Tips and Ideas:

Research sustainable and ethical brands to align with your values.

Experiment with different styles to discover what resonates with you.

Create a capsule wardrobe to simplify and refine your clothing choices.

Explore local markets and supermarkets

Practice mindful shopping by considering the quality and longevity of items.

Chapter 63: Automobile Interest

Description: Immerse yourself in the world of automobiles, whether through collecting classic cars, tinkering with engines, or simply appreciating the design and engineering of vehicles. Examples include restoring a vintage car, attending classic car shows, learning about the history and evolution of automobile technology.

Self-Assessment Questions:
How important is your interest in automobiles and related activities?

How satisfied are you with your current level of engagement in this area?

Tips and Ideas:
Attend car shows and exhibitions to admire different models.

Learn about automobile history, technology, and mechanics.

Join car enthusiast groups and forums to connect with like-minded individuals.

Experiment with DIY car projects to enhance your knowledge and skills.

Explore road trips to experience the joy of driving in different environments.

Chapter 64: Floral Interest

Description: Cultivate your love for flowers, whether through gardening, floral arrangement, or simply appreciating their vibrant colors and fragrances. Examples include creating a flower garden that blooms with different colors and varieties, attending floral arranging workshops to learn the art of creating stunning bouquets, exploring the symbolism of different flowers and their significance in various cultures.

Self-Assessment Questions:

How important is your passion for flowers and floral-related activities?

How satisfied are you with your current level of engagement with flowers?

Tips and Ideas:

Start a garden and experiment with growing different types of flowers.

Take floral arrangement workshops to create stunning bouquets.

Learn about the symbolism and cultural significance of various flowers.

Document your floral creations through photography or art.

Share your love for flowers by gifting arrangements to friends and family.

Chapter 65: Collector of Things

Description: Embrace the joy of collecting objects that hold sentimental value, whether it's stamps, coins, vintage toys, or any other items that spark your interest. Examples are building a collection of vintage postcards, gathering unique rocks and minerals from your travels, preserve childhood memories through collecting nostalgic toys and memorabilia.

Self-Assessment Questions:
How important is collecting items of value to you?
How satisfied are you with your current collection and its significance in your life?

Tips and Ideas:
Research and learn about the history and value of the items you collect.
Attend collector's fairs, conventions, and auctions to expand your collection.
Share your passion by displaying your collection in a creative and meaningful way.
Connect with other collectors to exchange knowledge and experiences.
Consider the stories behind each item, deepening the emotional connection.

Chapter 66: Repair, Fix, Restore, Rebuild, DIY

Description: Find fulfillment in repairing, restoring and rebuilding items, whether it's electronics, furniture, or everyday objects. Cultivate practical skills that empower you to breathe new life into the things you love. Examples include reviving old furniture pieces through refinishing, learning to mend clothing and textiles, fixing electronics and appliances, reducing waste and contributing to sustainability.

Self-Assessment Questions:

How important is the act of repairing and restoring things in your life?

How satisfied are you with your current level of repairing and restoring skills?

Tips and Ideas:

Take up DIY projects to practice repairing different types of items.

Join online communities and forums to seek advice and share experiences.

Learn about tools and techniques that enhance your repair abilities.

Collaborate with others on repair projects to exchange skills and ideas.

Offer your repair services to friends and family, contributing to sustainability.

Chapter 67: Astrology Interest

Description: Dive into the world of astrology, exploring the stars, planets, and their influence on personality traits and life events. Engage in horoscope readings, birth chart analysis, and cosmic contemplation. Examples include uncovering your birth chart, understanding the Feng Shui, engaging in daily horoscope.

Self-Assessment Questions:

How important is your interest in astrology and cosmic exploration?

How satisfied are you with your current level of knowledge and engagement in this area?

Tips and Ideas:

Study astrology to understand its principles and interpretations.

Explore your own birth chart and those of friends and family.

Keep a celestial journal to document your observations and reflections.

Attend Feng Shui workshops and seminars.

Engage in meditation and contemplation under celestial skies.

Chapter 68: Self-Care, Beauty, Wellness and Body Relaxation

Description: Delight in the realm of self-care, relaxation, and beauty. Immerse yourself in facial, body, wellness practices, and moments of tranquility that rejuvenate the body and soul. Examples include exploring beauty, self improvements, soothing scents, calming music and mindfulness.

Self-Assessment Questions:

How important is body beauty, self-care and relaxation to your overall well-being?

How satisfied are you with your current self-care and relaxation routines?

Tips and Ideas:

Create a serene environment at home for relaxation.

Explore various wellness practices such as meditation, yoga, and aromatherapy.

Schedule regular self-care beauty days to pamper yourself.

Discover spa retreats and wellness centers for immersive experiences.

Prioritize self-care as an essential aspect of your overall wellness journey.

Chapter 69: Fashion and Personal Style

Description: Fashion and Personal Style involve expressing creativity and identity through clothing and aesthetic choices. This circle empowers you to experiment with different styles, follow fashion trends, and curate a unique personal image. Examples include designing your clothing, exploring fashion history, and becoming a personal stylist.

Self-Assessment Questions:

How important is expressing your identity and creativity through fashion and personal style to you? (1-10)

How satisfied are you with your current level of engagement in fashion and cultivating your personal style? (1-10)

Tips and Ideas:

Experiment with different clothing styles, colors, and accessories to find your unique aesthetic.

Study fashion history and trends to gain inspiration and insights into the evolution of style.

Design and create your clothing or accessories to reflect your individuality.

Offer personal styling services to help others discover and enhance their personal style.

Attend fashion events, shows, and workshops to stay updated on the latest fashion innovations.

Chapter 70: Global Awareness and Positive Impact

Description: Global Awareness and Positive Impact involve addressing global issues and contributing to positive change on a larger scale. This circle empowers you to support international NGOs, volunteer for global initiatives, and engage in cross-cultural exchange. Examples include donating to global causes, participating in humanitarian missions, and promoting cultural understanding.

Self-Assessment Questions:
How important is making a positive impact on a global scale and fostering cross-cultural understanding to you? (1-10)

How satisfied are you with your current level of involvement in global awareness and international initiatives? (1-10)

Tips and Ideas:
Support international NGOs or charities that align with your values and causes.

Volunteer for global initiatives, such as disaster relief efforts or sustainable development projects.

Engage in cultural exchange programs or travel experiences to broaden your perspective.

Collaborate with individuals from diverse backgrounds to promote understanding and empathy.

Educate others about global issues and encourage responsible and ethical global citizenship.

Chapter 71: Model Building

Description: Dive into the world of model building, where creativity, attention to detail, and patience combine to create intricate and captivating miniature structures and scenes. Examples include building scale models of historical landmarks, vehicles, or architectural marvels. Exploring different materials and techniques, from plastic kits to paper models and beyond.

Self-Assessment Questions:
How important is model building to you?

How satisfied are you with your current level of engagement in model building?

Tips and Ideas:
Start with beginner-friendly kits to build confidence and develop skills.

Research historical accuracy and design principles to create authentic models.

Experiment with painting, weathering, and detailing techniques to enhance realism.

Share your creations with online communities and model building enthusiasts.

Use model building as a form of artistic expression and a way to channel your imagination.

Chapter 72: Bird Watching and Appreciation

Description: Embark on a journey of observing and appreciating birds in their natural habitats, experiencing the thrill of identifying different species and understanding their behaviors. Examples include equipping yourself with binoculars and field guides, visiting bird sanctuaries, nature reserves, and parks to observe a diverse range of avian life.

Self-Assessment Questions:

How important is bird watching and connecting with nature's avian inhabitants to you?

How satisfied are you with your current level of engagement in bird watching?

Tips and Ideas:

Join local bird-watching groups to learn from experienced enthusiasts.

Invest in a bird feeder or bird bath to attract birds to your backyard.

Learn to recognize bird calls and songs to enhance your identification skills.

Respect the habitats of birds and their environments while observing them.

Incorporate bird-friendly practices into your daily life to support conservation efforts.

Chapter 73: Magic and Illusion

Description: Delve into the captivating world of magic, where mystery, wonder, and skillful sleight of hand combine to create moments of astonishment and awe. Examples include learning and performing magic tricks that engage and amaze your audience.

Self-Assessment Questions:

How important is magic and the appreciation of illusion as a source of wonder to you?

How satisfied are you with your current level of engagement in magic and illusion?

Tips and Ideas:

Practice and refine your magic skills to become a skilled amateur magician.

Join magic clubs and communities to learn from experienced magicians.

Study the psychology and techniques behind different magic tricks.

Experiment with creating your own original magic routines.

Use magic as a form of entertainment to delight and surprise friends and family.

Chapter 74: Interior Decor and Home Improvement

Description: Explore the art of interior decor and home improvement, transforming your living spaces into reflections of your personal style and creating environments that nurture your well-being. Examples include experimenting with color schemes, furniture arrangements, and décor. Embarking on DIY home improvement projects that add value and personality to your home.

Self-Assessment Questions:
How important is interior decor and the improvement of your living spaces to your sense of comfort and identity?

How satisfied are you with your current living spaces and their alignment with your design preferences?

Tips and Ideas:
Research interior design principles and trends to guide your decor choices.

Set achievable home improvement goals and tackle them one project at a time.

Explore thrift stores and flea markets for unique decor items that tell your story.

Incorporate elements of functionality and organization into your design decisions.

Seek inspiration from design magazines, online platforms, and home improvement shows.

Chapter 75: Fishing Angling Interest

Description: Immerse yourself in the world of fishing, embracing the meditative aspects of angling, the thrill of the catch, and the connection with nature's aquatic wonders. Examples include learning different fishing techniques, from fly fishing in rivers to deep-sea fishing in the open ocean.

Self-Assessment Questions:
How important is your interest in fishing and the connection it offers with nature?

How satisfied are you with your current level of engagement in fishing?

Tips and Ideas:
Research fishing regulations and guidelines to ensure ethical and sustainable practices.

Learn about local fish species, their habitats, and feeding patterns.

Invest in appropriate fishing gear and equipment for different types of fishing.

Practice patience and mindfulness while waiting for the perfect catch.

Engage in fishing excursions with friends or family to create lasting memories.

Chapter 76: Watching Sports, Celebrating Team Spirit and Athletic Excellence

Description: Immerse yourself in the excitement of sports, from the camaraderie of cheering for your favorite teams to appreciating the dedication and skill of athletes. Examples attend live sports events to experience the energy and enthusiasm of the crowd, engaging in fantasy sports leagues and predictions to enhance your connection to the games.

Self-Assessment Questions:

How important is the act of watching sports and celebrating athletic achievements in your life?

How satisfied are you with your current level of engagement in sports-related activities?

Tips and Ideas:

Connect with fellow sports enthusiasts to share your passion and engage in friendly banter.

Host sports-watching parties to bring friends and family together for a shared experience.

Learn about the cultural significance of sports in different regions and societies.

Embrace sports as a form of entertainment, relaxation, and an opportunity for bonding.

Explore sports beyond your usual preferences to broaden your understanding and enjoyment.

Conclusion: Embrace Your Purposeful Journey

As we reach the culmination of "Finding Your Circles of Passion: Crafting a Purposeful Life," it is my hope that this exploration has ignited a flame of inspiration within you – a flame that will continue to burn brightly as you embark on your purposeful journey. Throughout the pages of this book, we have ventured into the depths of human experience, delving into the distinct circles that encompass the myriad facets of a life well-lived. We have traversed the realms of advocacy and artistry, technology and travel, relationships and self-discovery, each circle revealing a tapestry of possibilities waiting to be woven into the fabric of your existence.

The Tapestry of Your Life

Just as a tapestry is woven thread by thread, your life is crafted through the moments, choices, and intentions you infuse into each day. Your purposeful journey is not a linear path, but a rich and dynamic tapestry composed of the circles you engage with. These circles, these realms of passion and purpose, hold the power to shape your experiences, enrich your interactions, and leave an indelible mark on the world around you.

A Call to Action: Nurturing Your Circles

As we bid farewell to this book, I extend a heartfelt call to action – an invitation to nurture, cultivate, and amplify the Circles of Passion that resonate most deeply with your heart. It is within your power to turn the pages of inspiration into the chapters of your life story. The process begins by revisiting the circles that stirred your soul, assessing their importance, and reflecting on your current level of satisfaction. From there, the real magic unfolds as you take deliberate steps to enhance and expand your engagement with these circles.

Engage with intention. Seek opportunities to contribute, learn, and grow within the circles that align with your values and aspirations. Embrace the discomfort of growth, knowing that every challenge you overcome, every lesson you learn, enriches the tapestry of your purposeful journey.

Embrace Change and Adaptation

Throughout life's seasons, your Circles of Passion will evolve. As you transition through different life stages, new circles may emerge, while others may wane in significance. Embrace change with open arms, for it is through adaptation that we reveal the resilience of our purpose. Just as a tree sheds its leaves in autumn, only to bloom anew in spring, your purposeful journey is marked by cycles of growth, transformation, and renewal.

Leave a Legacy of Purpose

In the symphony of existence, your purposeful notes harmonize with the melodies of countless others. As you cultivate your Circles of Passion, remember that your contributions have the power to resonate far beyond the confines of your individual journey. Your advocacy can inspire change, your creativity can ignite passions, and your kindness can ripple through the lives of others. Embrace the knowledge that your legacy is not only the sum of your accomplishments but also the impact you leave upon the lives you touch.

B egin Your Next Chapter

As this book draws to a close, a new chapter in your purposeful journey unfolds. With every step you take, you are Crafting a Purposeful Life – one circle, one choice, one intention at a time. Embrace the adventure, savor the moments, and face each sunrise with the understanding that your purpose is a guiding star that will illuminate even the darkest of nights.

Thank you for embarking on this journey of self-discovery, reflection, and empowerment. Now, it is your turn to wield the pen and write the story of your purposeful life. May your journey be filled with passion, fulfillment, and a profound sense of purpose that lights up your path and inspires those who follow in your footsteps.

About the Author

Marako Marcus is a master storyteller, using his unique straight talk style of writing to provide practical tips and insights that can be applied in real life. He's on a mission to help people around the world, and to achieve this goal, he's releasing a series of bite-sized handbooks that are perfect for just-in-time reference.

What sets Marako apart is his ability to draw on over 25 years of experience as a management consultant and career coach. He's worked with organizations across the globe, developing people-centric interventions that bring diverse teams together and spark creative synergies.

As an author, Marako has published a number of books and articles on creativity and teamwork. He is also a popular speaker at conferences and events, captivating audiences with his engaging, humorous and thought-provoking presentations.

Marako is also an accomplished musician and composer, using his musical canvas to create stories and experiences that inspire relaxation, calmness, and creativity. You can find his music on all major streaming platforms, making it easy to enjoy whenever and wherever you need a moment of peace and inspiration!

Book Links available at https://linktr.ee/marakomarcusbooks